D1293952

BASKETBALL LEGENDS

Kareem Abdul-Jabbar
Charles Barkley
Larry Bird
Kobe Bryant
Wilt Chamberlain
Clyde Drexler
Julius Erving
Patrick Ewing
Kevin Garnett
Anfernee Hardaway
Tim Hardaway
The Head Coaches
Grant Hill
Juwan Howard
Allen Iverson
Magic Johnson
Michael Jordan
Shawn Kemp
Jason Kidd
Reggie Miller
Alonzo Mourning
Hakeem Olajuwon
Shaquille O'Neal
Gary Payton
Scottie Pippen
David Robinson
Dennis Rodman
John Stockton
Keith Van Horn
Antoine Walker
Chris Webber

CHELSEA HOUSE PUBLISHERS

KEITH
VAN HORN

Brent Kelley

Introduction by
Chuck Daly

CHELSEA HOUSE PUBLISHERS
Philadelphia

Produced by Combined Publishing, Inc.

CHELSEA HOUSE PUBLISHERS

Editor in Chief: Stephen Reginald
Managing Editor: James Gallagher
Production Manager: Pamela Loos
Art Director: Sara Davis
Director of Photography: Judy L. Hasday
Senior Production Editor: Lisa Chippendale
Publishing Coordinator: James McAvoy
Cover Design and Digital Illustrations: Keith Trego
Cover Photos: AP/Wide World Photos

The Chelsea House World Wide Web site address is
http://www.chelseahouse.com

First Printing

1 3 5 7 9 8 6 4 2

Library of Congress Cataloging-in-Publication Data

Kelley, Brent P.
    Keith Van Horn / Brent Kelley ; introduction by Chuck Daly.
       p. cm.—(Basketball legends)
    Includes bibliographical references and index.
    Summary: A biography of the determined star of the University
of Utah basketball team who became one of the top rookies in
the NBA in 1998.
    ISBN 0-7910-5009-2 (hc)
    1. Van Horn, Keith, 1975- —Juvenile literature. 2. Basketball players—
United States—Biography—Juvenile literature. [1. Van Horn, Keith, 1975- .
2. Basketball players.] I. Title. II. Series.
GV884.V365K45 1998
796.323'092—dc21
    [b]   98-45022
                                                                    CIP
                                                                    AC

CONTENTS

BECOMING A BASKETBALL LEGEND

Chuck Daly

What does it take to be a basketball superstar? Two of the three things it takes are easy to spot. Any great athlete must have excellent skills and tremendous dedication. The third quality needed is much harder to define, or even put in words. Others call it leadership or desire to win, but I'm not sure that explains it fully. This third quality relates to the athlete's thinking process, a certain mentality and work ethic. One can coach athletic skills, and while few superstars need outside influence to help keep them dedicated, it is possible for a coach to offer some well-timed words in order to keep that athlete fully motivated. But a coach can do no more than appeal to a player's will to win; how much that player is then capable of ensuring victory is up to his own internal workings.

In recent times, we have been fortunate to have seen some of the best to play the game. Larry Bird, Magic Johnson, and Michael Jordan had all three components of superstardom in full measure. They brought their teams to numerous championships, and made the players around them better. (They also made their coaches look smart.)

I myself coached a player who belongs in that class, Isiah Thomas, who helped lead the Detroit Pistons to consecutive NBA crowns. Isiah is not tall—he's just over six feet—but he could do whatever he wanted with the ball. And what he wanted to do most was lead and win.

All the players I mentioned above and those whom this series will chronicle are tremendously gifted athletes, but for the most part, you can't play professional basketball at all unless you have excellent skills. And few players get to stay on their team unless they are willing to dedicate themselves to improving their talents even more, learning about their opponents, and finding a way to join with their teammates and win.

It's that third element that separates the good player from the superstar, the memorable players from the legends of the game. Superstars know when to take over the game. If the situation calls for a defensive stop, the superstars stand up and do it. If the situation calls for a key pass, they make it. And if the situation calls for a big shot, they want the ball. They don't want the ball simply because of their own glory or ego. Instead they know—and their teammates know—that they are the ones who can deliver, regardless of the pressure.

The words "legend" and "superstar" are often tossed around without real meaning. Taking a hard look at some of those who truly can be classified as "legends" can provide insight into the things that brought them to that level. All of them developed their legacy over numerous seasons of play, even if certain games will always stand out in the memories of those who saw them. Those games typically featured amazing feats of all-around play. No matter how great the fans thought the superstars were, these players were capable of surprising the fans, their opponents, and occasionally even themselves. The desire to win took over, and with their dedication and athletic skills already in place, they were capable of the most astonishing achievements.

CHUCK DALY, now the head coach of the Orlando Magic, guided the Detroit Pistons to two straight NBA championships, in 1989 and 1990. He earned a gold medal as coach of the 1992 U.S. Olympic basketball team—the so-called "Dream Team"—and was inducted into the Pro Basketball Hall of Fame in 1994.

1

TURNING A
TEAM AROUND

The New Jersey Nets had a dismal 1996-97 season, compiling a 26-56 record in John Calipari's first season as head coach. The team finished 13th in the 15-team Eastern Conference, 43 games behind the champion Chicago Bulls. To make matters worse, the Nets' best player, All-Star forward Jayson Williams, didn't get along with Coach Calipari and demanded to be traded. The 1997-98 season looked bleak.

The Nets needed a good pick in the 1997 NBA draft of college players. They had two first round picks, number seven and number 21, but what they needed—a take-charge guy who could score and be a team leader—would be long gone by the time those numbers came around.

The San Antonio Spurs had the first pick, and they chose Wake Forest center Tim Duncan. Next to draft was the Philadelphia 76ers, and the team grabbed Keith Van Horn, the University of Utah

Keith Van Horn drives past Houston's Charles Barkley, giving all he has for his team.

All-American forward and three-time Western Athletic Conference Player-of-the-Year. Van Horn was the man Calipari and the Nets wanted.

In fact, the Nets had already put Van Horn through a pre-draft workout to see how good he really was. Nets assistant coach Kenny Gattison, a former NBA forward, guarded Van Horn and forced him to go to his left so he would have to use his left hand.

"What we wanted to see was if the guy could cross over and use his left hand and get by [Gattison]," explained Nets general manager John Nash.

Van Horn definitely could. He not only crossed over; he went by Gattison and dunked left handed.

Knowing that Van Horn would not be available by the time their seventh choice came up, the Nets arranged a trade with the 76ers. Philadelphia would take Van Horn with their pick, number two overall, and the two teams would make a trade.

Finally it came time for the Nets, and with the seventh choice they took Villanova University forward Tim Thomas. Then with pick number 21, they took guard Anthony Parker from Bradley University.

The trade was completed. The Nets sent guard Jim Jackson, center Eric Montross, and Thomas and Parker, their two first-round draft picks, to Philadelphia for Van Horn, guard Lucious Harris, forward Don McLean, and center Michael Cage.

The Nets' first order of business was to sign Van Horn to a solid contract for three years and approximately $9 million. Coach Calipari realized the significance of the contract.

"We are very pleased to sign Keith to a multi-

year deal," the coach said. "He's a superb out-side shooter and free-throw shooter and an excellent athlete. Keith's signing is another step forward in our efforts to put a top-caliber team on the floor."

In Van Horn's early days in the Nets' training camp, he so impressed team star Jayson Williams that Williams forgot his differences with Coach Calipari. "Cal," Williams said, "we got to make up. That's a franchise player out there."

Keith Van Horn holds a New Jersey Nets shirt at a news conference announcing his trade to the Nets after the 1997 NBA draft.

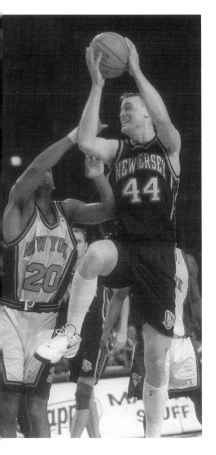

In a pre-season game against the New York Knicks, Keith drives toward the basket past Knicks guard Allan Houston.

In fact, the veteran Williams took more than a passing interest in the 22-year-old rookie.

"I'm his biggest fan," Jayson said. "Keith will be an All-Star next season. He's the smartest player I've ever played with, and he's such a good person. I've said he's the best player to come into the league since Michael Jordan, and I believe that. He can do it all. Right now, he's the best player this franchise ever had, except for Julius [Erving].

"I guarantee you he'll be an All-Star. My job is to protect him. My job is to put him under my wing on the court. I'm just not going to let nobody push him around." Williams's early opinion of the young man was only strengthened as pre-season games got under way.

After the first exhibition game, Van Horn was asked how he felt playing for the first time against the best basketball players in the world.

"I was real excited to get out there and play for real," he said. "It's different, playing against people you watched play on television all your life."

As the pre-season schedule went along, it was obvious that Van Horn was more than ready for NBA basketball. Frank Layden, former coach of the NBA's Utah Jazz, had seen him play many times in college. Layden wasn't at all surprised by how well Van Horn performed when he started playing with the Nets at the Brendan Byrne Arena in East Rutherford, New Jersey.

"They [the Nets] are almost getting a seasoned veteran out of college," Layden said. "He's been through so much coaching and fundamentals. He's seen a lot and been in big games."

Keith would get a lot of opportunities to play, Layden predicted. And the rookie would find a way to play effectively in the NBA, he said.

As the start of the season approached, Van Horn was becoming the key to the Nets' offense. He was being compared to such basketball greats as Larry Bird and Michael Jordan, his boyhood hero.

Both the Nets and the fans were expecting great things from him, but when asked what he expected of himself, Van Horn modestly replied, "I really don't have any expectations going into the season. The only expectations I have for myself is to go out and play hard every night. I feel if I do that, I will be successful. I still have to work on my overall game. I'm not the player I want to be right now. I think I've got a lot of improvement that's possible. I'm going out and work hard every day to do that."

One of Van Horn's goals involved the whole team.

"I would like to see this team in the playoffs. I think it's definitely an attainable goal. That's really the only goal I've set either for myself or for this team," he explained. "I'm going to deal with whatever situation is handed to me, whether they're going to make me the go-to guy this season or make me sit and follow what the older guys do. That's their decision. I'm going to be happy and deal with whatever is handed to me."

By the time the pre-season schedule was almost over, he had indeed become the go-to guy. He impressed everyone who saw him, but as the season opener neared, things took a bad turn. In late October 1997, Van Horn severely sprained his right ankle in an exhibition game against the Cleveland Cavaliers and was nearly unable to walk. Running, twisting, and pivoting were out of the question.

Van Horn was forced to miss the first 17 games

Keith's injury kept him out for the beginning of his first season. He played his first NBA game here against the 76ers in December 1997.

of the season, and when he was finally able to play, the ankle was still painful. The injury required rest and a lot of time to heal fully, but Van Horn knew the Nets were paying him to play. So he played.

His first NBA game, on December 5, 1997, was

against the 76ers, the team that drafted him. Playing part-time in that game, he scored 11 points as the Nets won, 107-88.

Coach Calipari was very pleased. "It was a good shooting night for him, and he didn't get embarrassed on defense. He's going to learn about the fouls, but he showed us what he's capable of."

As it turns out, Van Horn showed he was capable of leading the team in scoring and averaged more minutes played per game than any other rookie in the league, even with his ankle still bothering him. At the All-Star break, he was chosen to play in the Schick Rookie Game. He scored 17 points against the best rookies and pulled down 10 rebounds, tops in the game. And in a charity contest before the game, he bested number one draft pick Tim Duncan in a one-on-one freestyle shooting competition.

A broken toe on his right foot sidelined Van Horn for three games shortly after the All-Star break. In his first game back, he showed no ill effects as he scored a team-high 19 points in a 93-87 win over the Orlando Magic. The teamwork of Van Horn and Williams, paired with Coach Calipari's leadership, worked well. And the Nets, who won only 26 games in the 1996-97 season, had won 27 games by the All-Star break in the 1997-98 season.

The lowly Nets of the previous year were suddenly playoff contenders.

2

BORN TO BASKETBALL

Areporter once asked Van Horn how long he had been playing basketball. He thought for a few seconds, then answered, "Since the first moments of my life that I can remember, basketball was involved in it. I never imagined life without basketball."

Van Horn was born October 23, 1975, in Diamond Bar, California, an upper middle-class suburb of Los Angeles. He was the youngest of three children of Kenneth and May Van Horn.

He was destined to be a big man. Ken, his dad, was 6'8" tall and weighed 230 pounds. And he was destined to play basketball. Ken had played at Lincoln High School and had built a small basketball court for his kids next to the family home.

Keith got his first basketball before he can remember. Some babies are given rattles or stuffed animals; Keith was given a small basketball.

When he became a toddler, he carried around his ball and learned to bounce it. He would sit and watch the big kids shoot baskets and play games on the family court. He wanted to play,

Keith Van Horn laughs during the press conference announcing the dream of an eight-year-old had come true—he would be playing in the NBA for the New Jersey Nets.

too, but he was too small and too young to join in.

Eventually the bigger kids let Keith try to shoot. His sister Kim, nine years older and a fine athlete, began playing one-on-one games with her little brother. It was always one-sided, and Kim came out on top every time for years.

Keith didn't give up, though, and those games against Kim helped him become the terror of his age group. In elementary and junior high school, none of the other boys could touch him on the basketball court. The fact that he was taller than everyone else helped, of course, but he was also quicker and more agile than the other kids.

He was born with great talent, but without practice that talent would never have been developed. But Keith practiced. Day and night, winter and summer, rain or shine. If there was a basketball court nearby, he was there. As the sports seasons changed, his friends switched from basketball to baseball, then from baseball to football. Keith didn't switch. He stuck with basketball.

Ken, his dad, worked with him a lot, showing him moves and shots and ball-handling tricks. Some boys don't learn, but Keith did. He was always eager to pick up a new basketball skill.

One day when he was eight, he was out on the family court shooting baskets and making most of them. Jump shots, layups, free throws—one after another, the ball went through the hoop.

When it came time to quit for the day, he tucked the ball under his arm and went in the house. He found his mother in the kitchen. He looked her right in the eye and announced, "I've decided to play in the NBA."

First, though, came youth leagues and summer programs. He starred in all of them. He was at an age when a lot of kids were dropping out of sports because they required too much time, or because practice was too hard, or because they took away from television time, or because they interfered with their interest in the opposite sex, or simply because they were too much work.

Keith began playing basketball harder than ever.

3
HIGH SCHOOL RECORD SETTER

Shortly before he turned 14, Keith entered Diamond Bar High School. Well over six feet tall and thin as a rail, he was easy to spot walking through the corridors.

That year, he accomplished something that had eluded him all his life: he finally defeated his older sister Kim in one-on-one basketball. Kim, who was 23 at the time, had been a volleyball player at the University of Southern California and was an excellent athlete. For years, she had easily beaten her little brother on the basketball court, but no more.

When it came time for high school basketball tryouts, Keith was there along with several other outstanding young athletes. The nephew of the great Wilt Chamberlain was in the group of freshmen, as was the son of former Major League Baseball All-Star George Hendrick.

Bill Murray was Diamond Bar's basketball coach. He was a seasoned veteran with more than 20 years of high school coaching experience, over a decade of it at Diamond Bar. He had

Keith's high school coach worried that the tall skinny kid who tried out for his team was too frail to play basketball—but he soon realized he had a star on his hands.

seen hundreds of high school basketball hopefuls come and go. A 14-year-old as tall as Keith would have interested any basketball coach, and Murray was no exception, but height seemed to be Keith's only asset. He was painfully thin, gangly almost to the point of awkwardness, and pale as a ghost.

After watching the youngster for a few days, Murray wasn't greatly impressed. He thought he looked "interesting, but nothing special." His opinion changed rapidly, however. Murray soon

Growing up, Keith had idolized Michael Jordan, and he realized a childhood dream when he played on the same court as Jordan in the NBA.

realized the gangly kid had ability he had rarely seen.

Other than tending to his schoolwork, basketball was all Keith did. As his close friend Blake Johnstone said, "Basketball was his girlfriend."

Because of the goal he set for himself as an eight-year-old—to play in the National Basketball Association—Keith devoted himself to basketball. During the summers, when his friends would go to the beach or have summer jobs or just hang out, Keith played basketball any time he could and anywhere—pickup games at schoolyards, on his home court, in junior leagues.

His bedroom was a shrine to basketball, or rather to Michael Jordan. Jordan was Keith's idol; his walls were lined with pictures and posters of his hero. Keith dreamed of playing alongside him with the Chicago Bulls.

When he was 16, Keith got his driver's license and a red pickup truck. This widened his basketball horizons. He and his buddy Blake, who was only 14, would leave at seven in the morning to go looking for games. They drove to wherever someone might be playing basketball— parks, schools, inner city Los Angeles, even to colleges to take on players several years older than they were.

Keith and Blake would go to a court where some guys they didn't know were playing and ask if they could join them. Blake, outgoing and talkative as well as a muscular 5'9" tall, would be readily accepted, but Keith, although taller than the others, was quiet and so pale and thin that he looked as if he would break. They looked at him with skepticism.

Often, the others would look at him and say, "No, I don't think so." It was up to Blake, who is

African American, to convince them to let the shy, quiet, white boy play. Once they did, it took only a few minutes for them to decide Keith knew how to play.

Blake remembers. "He'd do stuff in parks that would blow your mind. Stuff like cross-overs or throwing it back over his head. He was like the silent assassin. People would say all the time, 'Dang, he plays like a brother. He plays like he's black.'"

When Keith returned home after these games, his father, always supportive, was interested in how he had played. It was the first thing he asked Keith when he came in the house.

By the time Keith was 16, Coach Murray realized he was the best player he had ever coached. And he was still growing—approaching 6'7". Although he was still gangly and gave the impression that he had to be clumsy and awkward, Keith's coordination and athletic ability on the court seemed to grow right along with his height.

Others began to notice the tall, skinny teenager because of his total basketball ability. He was not just a tall kid who could score by jumping over his shorter opponents. He was a complete player. He could dribble and drive. He blocked shots. He made great passes. And he was a team player; winning was more important than his personal stats.

Coach Murray remembered how Keith put the team first. "Something that really sticks out in my mind was between his junior and senior years," the coach recalled. "Keith didn't go to any of those summer basketball camps where all those college and NBA scouts are. He stayed with us so we'd be better. It takes a pretty special person to sacrifice himself for the good of the team."

As a senior, Keith was named team captain. As captain, he had the right to choose the shoes the team wore. Michael Jordan endorsed Nike, and if Nike was good enough for Michael, Nike was good enough for Keith. No other brand was even considered.

Coach Murray was a great help in Keith's development. He cared about his players. He'd open the gym at sunrise for the team members. He made sure the boys did their schoolwork, and he helped them if they needed it. He personally took his players to 3-on-3 tournaments on his days off. He was their friend.

Keith lived for the team. His friend Blake said, "You know, I don't even know if he went to the prom. He'd do anything for the game because he loved playing so much."

As a senior, Keith had reached 6'8" and was leading the Diamond Bar Brahmas to the possibility of a Sierra League championship. It went down to the last second of the last game of the season, against arch-rival Ayala. With seconds left, Keith blocked a shot, recovered the ball, dribbled the length of the court, and was fouled on his shot attempt as time ran out. With no time left, he calmly sank the two free throws, giving Diamond Bar the championship.

Keith became the top single-season scorer in school history, averaging 29.2 points a game. Also, he took down 10.1 rebounds, dished out 3.7 assists, and blocked 4 shots per game. And he set a school record for points in one game with 46.

Everyone had noticed him by this time. He was named to numerous All-Star teams and given several honors. He was named to the All-State first team in California, an honor that takes

University of Utah coach Rich Majerus knew he wanted Van Horn for his team as soon as he saw him play.

on greater significance because California has more high school basketball players than any other state in the country. He was also named to the California Interscholastic Federation first team and the All-Western United States first team.

He was voted the San Gabriel Valley Player of the Year and the Inland Valley Player of the Year. To top it all off, the school retired his number.

His number 44 jersey now hangs in a place of honor in the school gymnasium.

Along the way, many college scouts took notice of Keith. He was most interested in Utah, California, and Arizona State, and each of those schools pursued him heavily.

Utah coach Rick Majerus sent assistant coach Donny Daniels to see Keith play. One day, he watched him in a pickup game at Ronald Reagan Park in Diamond Bar. "Keith was humiliating the competition," he said. "He was draining 20-footers from all over the court. I was sitting on a park bench with some of the locals and all they kept saying was, 'That white boy can play!'"

Keith liked Daniels and also liked Majerus when they met. And Coach Daniels was so impressed with Keith that he once attended a Diamond Bar game even though he knew Keith wouldn't be playing because of a wrist injury. He just wanted to watch him watch.

With the prospect of a lot of playing time as a freshman, Keith decided to attend the University of Utah.

4

OFF TO COLLEGE

Keith was still several weeks short of his 18th birthday when he left home to travel hundreds of miles to attend the University of Utah in Salt Lake City. The transition from high school to college can be tough. For Keith, lots of studying and good grades were expected. But he was also expected to excel in basketball.

Ken, his father, knew his son was good and hoped an NBA contract was in his future. But he asked Keith to promise to stay in college and earn his degree so there would be something to fall back on if professional basketball didn't work out. Keith made the promise to his father.

Before his freshman year actually began, Keith met the basketball squad and the coaches, so he wasn't a total stranger on the first day of school in fall 1993. On the second day, however, he met someone who would make more of a difference in his life than anyone ever had.

At a bonfire party for incoming students, Keith got to know another freshman, a young woman from the Salt Lake City suburb of Sandy, Utah.

Keith put all his energy into playing for his college team just as he had for his high school team. Basketball is what he loves to do.

Her name was Amy Sida, and they hit it off right away and began dating.

Classes got underway, and Keith adjusted well. When basketball practices began, Keith played well against the older players offensively, but there were a few problems on defense.

"He showed up here at 190 pounds and thin as a thermometer," Coach Majerus said, "so at the beginning, the way the guys moved past him it was like opening Boulder Dam."

But no one worked harder, both on the court and in the weight room. His defense still needed work, but he added bulk and muscle to his frame so no one could push him around anymore.

The Utes had problems in the 1993-94 season, although Keith himself played brilliantly. Three other starters were lost to the team early. One was injured, one was suspended, and one quit the team. Another team member, forward Tony Horn, was unhappy with his playing time and told everyone that he, not Keith, should be in the starting lineup.

Then on January 25, 1994, at 2 A.M., there was a knock on Keith's dormitory room door. It was Coach Majerus, delivering a message from Keith's mother, May, in California.

Keith's father had died of a heart attack in his sleep, and Mrs. Van Horn had asked the coach to break the news to Keith and help him. Majerus understood; he had had to do the same thing with five other players over the years, and his own dad had passed away three years earlier.

The coach took Keith to an all-night restaurant, and the two talked the rest of the night. They told each other stories about their fathers, and during that long night a bond was formed between the player and the coach that remains strong.

The next morning, Keith flew home to California and missed the Utes' next three games. He returned in time for a game with the University of Wyoming, which Utah lost. During that game, the events of the past several months began weighing on his mind.

"Everything—my dad's death, our losing, the team dissension—finally overcame me. I wondered if I should even have come back this season. I almost broke down right on the court," Keith said.

Immediately after the game, he headed to a restroom stall and "bawled like a baby," as he

Keith was the star of Utah's team for the four years he played there, winning numerous awards and titles throughout his college years.

described it. It was apparently what he needed to do. Over the next five games, he averaged 26 points.

In spite of Keith's brilliant play, Utah managed only a 14-14 record. But even on a mediocre team, he was recognized.

He was the first freshman in 21 years (Ticky Burden was the last before him, in the 1972-73 season) to lead the team in scoring (18.3 points per game). For this and his excellent overall play, he was named the Western Athletic Conference (WAC) Freshman of the Year and selected for the WAC first team. He was also first-team All-Newcomer and named to the All-District team by the United States Basketball Writers Association.

Roger Reid, the head basketball coach at Brigham Young University (BYU), was among those most impressed by the freshman phenom at his team's arch rival school. "I've been in this league for 18 years and I don't think there's been any finer player in our league for a long, long time," said the man who had coached the great Danny Ainge back in the '70s.

Through all the good times and bad times of the freshman year, Amy Sida was there. They were still dating.

As Keith's sophomore year began, everything seemed to be falling into place. He had come to grips with the loss of his father, the team dissension seemed to be a thing of the past, some new freshmen had joined the team, and the season ahead held great promise. And he and Amy were in love.

The season got underway, and Coach Majerus molded his players into a unit that only got better with each game. Keith as an individual also improved each time out. Twice during the course of the season, he was named WAC Player of the Week, first for his games against New Mexico and the University of Texas at El Paso (UTEP), and then for his play versus Wyoming and Colorado State.

Utah won the regular-season WAC championship, and the team celebrated by having a city-wide party, except for Keith and Coach Majerus. The coach went to a family restaurant off the freeway in Salt Lake City, and about an hour later in walked Keith with his mother, some other relatives, and some family friends.

"I'll never forget that night because Keith could have been prince of the city, but he chose to celebrate with his family, eating ice cream sundaes with a bunch of people twice his age," the coach said.

After the regular season ended, the WAC tournament began. The Utes capped a brilliant season with the tournament crown, and Keith was named to the All-Tournament team and tournament Most Valuable Player.

He was also named WAC Player of the Year, leading the conference in scoring (21.9) and rebounds (10.1). Overall, including non-conference games, he averaged 21 points and 8.5 rebounds, both tops on the team. And he led the WAC in free-throw shooting, making 85.6 percent of his shots.

He was named District Player of the Year and first team All-WAC. He was gaining recognition as one of the top professional prospects in the country.

Keith accomplished so much in the basketball arena, but a private matter was weighing on his mind. Amy was pregnant. Both she and Keith were only 19 and unsure of what the future held for them, for school, for basketball, and for their coming baby. They were engaged, but they decided not to get married. Yet.

The baby wasn't due until after the end of the basketball season, and on May 29, 1995, Amy went into labor. Keith wasn't ready. It was final exam week, and he had a take-home test—a written paper—due the next day. He hadn't even started it.

He went to the hospital with Amy at about five in the evening, taking his study materials with him. "I just wrote [the paper] in the delivery room. Brought in about four books and a few pens and loose-leaf paper," he recalled. "Sabrina was born at about 1:30 a.m. on May 30, and later I went home and typed up the paper. Had to have it in by 4 p.m."

He got an A. "Amy was due, the paper was due. Coach Majerus really gets on our case about academics," he said, matter-of-factly explaining how he handled both deadlines.

Baby Sabrina meant more responsibility for Keith, although he and Amy still weren't sure whether they were going to get married. They broke off their engagement and didn't see each other for a while. During that time, Keith began thinking about his father, how much he meant to him, and how important it was to have a strong family life. He wanted Sabrina to have that, and he knew he loved Amy.

On Christmas Eve 1995, he got down on his knees and proposed again. Amy accepted again, but no date was set for the wedding.

It was Keith's junior year. As the basketball season got underway, there were big predictions for both the team and its star. And the people doing the predicting were not disappointed.

The Utes won the WAC championship again, and at one point were ranked number two in the nation. The big reason, of course, was Keith, who was the most dominating player in the conference.

For the second year in a row, he was named WAC Player of the Week twice, first for his games with UTEP and New Mexico and then for his 38-point outbreak against BYU at Provo, the home of BYU.

He led the team in scoring (21.9) and rebounds (8.8) again. And again he was named to numerous All-Star teams: All-WAC, All-District, WAC All-Tournament, etc. He was named the 1996 Deseret News Athlete of the Year and the 1996 Utah M. S. Male Athlete of the Year, and he won the Joe Kearney Award as the WAC's top male athlete. He was a finalist for three of college basketball's most prestigious honors: the John Wooden Award, the RCA Player of the Year Award, and the Naismith Player of the Year Award. And for the second straight year, Keith was named WAC Player of the Year.

Everyone had heard of him now, especially the NBA. Rumors began circulating that he would leave school and enter the professional draft, skipping his senior year.

The public's curiosity surrounding his basketball career was relentless. One day, as he was sitting in a McDonald's preparing to eat three QuarterPounders, a man came up to him and said, "So, are you going pro? Don't think I don't know who you are."

Van Horn shook the man's hand and assured him he planned to return to college for his senior year.

"People come up to me and say they heard I'm

leaving," he said at the time.

Van Horn had made his decision to stay in school after a heart-to-heart talk with Coach Majerus a week after the season's last game. The talk went something like this:

"What kind of car do you want?" asked the coach.

"A Lexus," replied Van Horn.

"What kind of house do you want?"

"A house with a swimming pool."

"What does Amy want?"

"She wants to go to nursing school."

"What do you want for Sabrina?"

"A stroller she can't escape from."

The coach told Van Horn about the "Al McGuire Refrigerator Theory," which goes something like this: "The less one has in one's refrigerator, the more avidly one should seek wealth." He said to Van Horn, "I look in your refrigerator, and you're lucky if you've got a quart of milk."

Majerus also told Van Horn he would probably be one of the top 10 picks and become an instant millionaire.

So his coach—one of his closest friends—had told him to take the money and run, instead of finishing his senior year at Utah.

Another close friend seconded the idea. Greg Riolo, Van Horn's roommate, told him, "I'd leave in a heartbeat if millions of dollars were staring me in the face."

But then Keith reminded them of his promise to his dad. He would graduate.

He summed it up by saying, "I don't want to worry about whether I'm going to get my degree

Wake Forest center Tim Duncan, right, tries to shoot over Utah forward Keith Van Horn.

Keith and Coach Majerus announce his decision to stay at college for his senior year instead of going to the NBA.

10 years down the road. I want to get it finished up." And to show his team-oriented mindset, he added, "Besides, I think that we're going to have a great team next year, and I want to be around for it. I love this group of guys that we have, and I love playing with them."

Still, there was pressure to enter the draft. But Keith steadfastly held his ground. "I'll do what I say I'm going to do," he said. "Anybody that talks to me, I'll tell them what I'm about and who I am. I'm not the type of person to hide anything."

And that was it. A promise to his father and a desire to help the Utes to a big season in his senior year kept him in school. The millions of dollars had to wait.

But Amy didn't have to wait. She and Keith were married in August 1996 as Keith spent the summer helping Coach Majerus run his basketball camp for kids. It didn't pay millions of dollars.

In fact, it paid nothing.

5

UTAH'S ALL-
TIME BEST

Shortly before the fall term of Van Horn's senior year, the pre-season All-America selections were announced. His name was there; in fact, one publication called him "the top power forward in the country."

As practice got underway, he was the center of attention on the Utes' basketball team. There were reporters and photographers from the college and local newspapers and TV stations, of course, but there were also many representatives of the national media.

Balancing the notoriety with the pressures of school and family was a challenge. As the season began, it looked as if it was more than Van Horn could handle. After the first five games, he was making only a little more than one-third of his shots, a far cry from his first three years, in which he made more than half of his shots. The low point was reached in the team's fifth game, against sixth-ranked Arizona, when he hit only three of 12 field-goal attempts and scored just 15 points as the Utes lost for the first time that season, 69-61.

Keith Van Horn drives past Kentucky's Jamaal Magloire in the NCAA regional championship game in March 1997.

But then he came out of his slump. In the game after Arizona, against Weber State, he led Utah to an 83-47 romp with his career high of 41 points. He pulled down a personal season-high 15 rebounds and was named WAC Player of the Week for his efforts.

He followed that a week later with 34 points and 12 rebounds in an 80-68 victory over a tough Texas team, earning his second straight Player of the Week honor. Whatever had bothered him earlier was obviously gone. Later, for games against BYU and Colorado State, he earned his third Player of the Week award.

Rick Majerus, his friend as well as his coach, was his greatest booster. "He's a beautiful person," he said. "He's kind, he's sensitive, he's a '90s kind of guy, a renaissance guy. He's a good friend to have. He's almost too good to be true."

There may have been a point early in the season when Van Horn questioned his decision not to turn pro. He had an interview scheduled and his pickup truck, now nearly 10 years old, would not start, and he was late. He denied any second thoughts, though, saying with a smile, "Yeah, a Lexus probably would have an extra battery, but I have no regrets about staying."

His fondness for his coach also helped him to overcome any second thoughts. "He's always said he likes me better as a person than a basketball player. A lot of what he teaches on the basketball floor translates to everyday life. He's talked about how hard work and discipline will carry you through."

The hard work, in fact, caused Majerus to worry a little. "I have to call him aside sometimes and tell him, 'Keith, make sure you're enjoying

Keith was aggressive and hardworking on defense. His move here was called a foul.

all this.' He wants to learn, he enjoys being challenged."

Van Horn said he simply has priorities. "God, family, and work—and work hard at whatever you do." Shortly before the first game, the work from studying, classes, and basketball practice was overwhelming him.

Coach Majerus remembered a conversation they had in late October. "He worried about having time to take his daughter trick-or-treating on Halloween, and she's only two. That's the kind of guy he is."

He found the time for trick-or-treating, and he worked out his early-season problems on the court, too. After the Weber State game, he said, "I feel comfortable now. It's just a game and a very small part of life, but it's something I love."

The Utes lost again on New Year's Eve in their 10th game, 70-59, to highly ranked Wake Forest, and four days later conference play began. With Van Horn averaging 20 points a game, Utah breezed through the first seven games before running into a super-hyped University of New Mexico. Utah was trounced badly, 87-71, despite Van Horn's 28 points and team-high seven rebounds.

That was the team's last defeat of the regular season as they ran off eight straight wins, including a runaway 78-58 rematch with New Mexico five days before the WAC tournament began. Two weeks earlier, Van Horn had scored 40 as the Utes had their highest point total of the season in a 94-91 victory over Texas Christian University (TCU).

The tournament began against the lowly Southern Methodist University Mustangs, who had fallen twice to Utah by a total of 38 points already that season. In those two previous games, the Mustangs had held Van Horn down, but they couldn't stop him when it came to tournament time. Van Horn scored at the buzzer as the Utes barely edged SMU, 59-58. His 25 points were high for the game.

The next day the foe was the tough New Mex-

Keith reaches high over the heads of the opposing team to help bring his team to victory.

ico Lobos again. Considering that they were the last team to down the Utes, the Lobos had high hopes of pulling off a major upset. They made a game of it, but Utah prevailed at the end, 72-70, as Van Horn once again scored the game-winning points at the buzzer. Scoring honors went to teammate Andre Miller with 21 points, but Keith pulled down 10 rebounds.

It was beginning to look like Utah was past its peak and might not win the WAC tournament for the first time since Van Horn's freshman year. The next day was another tough opponent. TCU had lost the two regular season games with Utah but only by a total of seven points, and they had given Utah the toughest time of any WAC team. The Horned Frogs' downfall, however, had been Van Horn. He had scored 63 points against them and taken down 24 rebounds in those two games, and there was no stopping him in this tournament game either. Van Horn was a one-man wrecking crew, scoring 37 points and taking 15 rebounds as the Utes breezed, 89-68. It was the team's 11th win in a row.

Utah entered the NCAA Tournament six days later as the number two ranked team in the country, although they were only seeded second in the West Region. Their opponent in the opening round of play was 15th-seeded Navy, a team that had won nine straight games.

But the Midshipmen were no match for the taller, quicker, more agile Utes, and the 75-61 final was not as close as the score made it seem. Van Horn dominated the boards with 11 rebounds and scored 16 points, while teammate Michael Doleac topped the team with 19.

Because his team was in such command, Coach Majerus was able to rest his starters during the second half, and Van Horn spent as much time on the bench as he did on the court. He realized the importance of this. "It was good for our starters and players who play a lot to get some rest," he said after the game.

Two days later, the Utes faced the University of North Carolina, Charlotte, the seventh seed and upset winner over perennial powerhouse Georgetown. Van Horn scored 16 points in the first half and finished with 27 and added eight rebounds as the Utes once again dominated their opponent. The final score was 77-58.

Next came sixth-seeded Stanford, and it may have been Utah's toughest game of the year to that point. The Utes prevailed, 82-77, but it took an overtime period without Van Horn to do it. After being ahead by 16 points in the first half, Utah faltered after the intermission, and Stanford came back to tie it at 67 at the end of regulation play.

Van Horn picked up his fifth foul just 34 seconds into overtime and had to take his 25 points to the bench. Stanford's Brevin Knight, who made the basket that tied the game, made the first of his two free throws after the foul and gave his team its only lead of the day at 68-67.

Van Horn talked to his teammates during a timeout. "I told them I had confidence in them, and they should have confidence in themselves. This is not a one-man team, and we proved it tonight," Keith explained later.

The next opponent, two days later, was the University of Kentucky, a team Utah had always had trouble with. This game was no exception, and Kentucky won, 72-59. Down 34-24 at halftime, the Utes rallied to tie it at 43-all midway in the second half, but the Wildcats' depth and quickness were too much for them.

Van Horn led Utah with 15 points but was not able to play his game. "I really was never able to get in an offensive flow just because every time I tried to come off a screen they just switched out on me, so I never really was able to get the ball a whole lot. Kentucky had the athletes to do that," he said after the game. He had only 12 shots from the floor and made five, as the Utes fell short of the Final Four, which they had last reached way back in 1966.

And that ended Utah's season and Van Horn's college career. Both had been very successful. The Utes finished with a record of 29-4, and Van Horn was named to six All-America first teams.

He became the first player in history to be named WAC Player of the Year for three straight years, he was first team All-WAC for the fourth year, and he was named District Player of the Year for the third year in a row. He was named the WAC tournament MVP for the second time and named to the WAC All-Defensive team. And once again he was a finalist for the top awards for college basketball players.

He led the WAC in free throw percentage (90.4), and he led Utah in scoring (22.0) and rebounds (9.5).

And he ended his career as the top scorer in both Utah and WAC history, surpassing Billy "The Hill" McGill and Danny Ainge, respectively, with 2,542 points.

The four years of college, the loss of his father, and becoming a father himself as well as a husband had all worked to help Van Horn mature into a good person as well as a great basketball player. "Four years ago when I was coming into college, I was just thinking basketball, basketball, basketball. Four years later, I was thinking more about school, family, and things that were not on the top of my priority list before," he said, referring to his personal growth.

His maturity impressed the NBA teams, and Van Horn knew that. "A lot of NBA people realize that what you do off the court affects what you do on the court," he said.

Frank Layden, president of the NBA's Utah Jazz, agreed. "He's a big man who can run, jump, post up, and shoot threes, and he's clutch at the foul line, but more important, he does all that with a very even temperament. Keith is the Clark Kent of college basketball. There's an S somewhere underneath his jersey."

His number 44 was retired by Utah, just as it was four years earlier by Diamond Bar High School. He had played basketball at two levels of scholastic competition and had been the best both schools had ever had.

Now it was time to show what he could do in the NBA.

6

REACHING HIS GOAL

The only goal Van Horn set at the beginning of his rookie NBA season was to attempt to help the Nets reach the playoffs. The team had last been involved in postseason play four seasons earlier in 1994, and going into the 1997-98 season, the odds were very much against them making it to the playoffs.

Even without Van Horn for the first 17 games due to his injured ankle, the Nets looked better than they had the previous year. When Van Horn joined them, it was like a shot in the arm. The hapless Nets of 1996-97 could suddenly hold their own with anyone.

By mid-season, they looked as if they were legitimate contenders for a playoff spot. When they ran off five straight wins shortly after the All-Star break, even the doubters started to believe, but then things seemed to fall apart.

As quickly as the winning streak began, it ended, and they lost 10 of their next 12, including seven in a row. They began looking like the old Nets.

They fell out of contention for a playoff berth,

Keith was drafted into the NBA by the Philadelphia 76ers and then traded to the New Jersey Nets.

and their prospects were bleak. Van Horn's scoring had fallen off, and he was not shooting well. Jayson Williams was in and out of the lineup due to injuries.

Then, just as suddenly as the team had declined, it turned around again. And so did Van Horn. For the final month of the season, he played better than he had ever played in his life.

In early April, the Nets reeled off another five wins in a row and moved right back into contention for a spot in the playoffs. In fact, it looked as if they might end up with the second best record in their division and avoid having to play the mighty Chicago Bulls in the first round of the playoffs.

But it was not to be; the up-and-down roller coaster ride wasn't over yet. They lost three in a row, and it came down to the last game of the regular season. If they won, they were in the playoffs. If they lost, the players all went home for the summer.

Everyone on the team knew what was at stake, and they were all up for the game against the Detroit Pistons. It was the first time since December the two teams had faced each other. In their three previous meetings, the Pistons had won twice.

This game was all New Jersey, however, as the Nets won, 114-101. For the first time since 1994, they were in the playoffs. Van Horn scored 25 points and averaged 25 down the stretch, when the team needed him the most.

Unfortunately, they were matched up against the Bulls, perhaps the greatest team ever. In

Chicago Bull Scott Burrell dives to try to beat Van Horn to a loose ball in an NBA playoff game.

their four meetings during the regular season, Chicago had taken each game and only one had even been close. To make matters worse, the first two games of the best-of-five series were in Chicago. Van Horn would be going head-to-head with Michael Jordan, his idol, in the most important games he had ever played.

The series began on April 24, and the Nets were not at full force. In fact, their three top stars were ailing for one reason or another. Jayson Williams, their leading rebounder, insisted on playing, but lingering injuries kept him from being 100 percent. Sam Cassell, their leading assist man and second leading scorer, was also hampered by injury.

And Van Horn was suffering from a stomach virus. He probably wasn't even playing at 50 percent. Still, he scored 10 points and took four rebounds in the first half, which ended with the Bulls leading by only four points. But he was too weak and too sick to play after the intermission. He played only 16 minutes, less than half the time he usually put in, during the entire game.

But even without Van Horn, the Nets played tough. Trailing by 10 after the third period, they rallied in the fourth quarter to tie it at 89 and force an overtime.

The healthier and more experienced Bulls outscored them, 7-4, in the overtime period to take the game, 96-93, putting the Nets down, one game to none.

Game two was played two days later. Van Horn

Chicago Bull Dennis Rodman celebrates a basket as he runs past Van Horn in the final game of the 1997-98 season for the Nets.

Philadelphia 76er Terry Cummings and Van Horn compete under the net.

was over his bout with the stomach virus, but it had weakened him, and now Cassell had the bug.

Van Horn averaged more than 37 minutes a game during the season, but this game he was only able to put in 29 and again scored only 10 points, as the Jordan-led Bulls won another close one, 96-91.

The teams were back in New Jersey for the third game on April 29, but it didn't matter as Jordan scored 38 points. Chicago led all the way, winning 116-101. Van Horn was back in form, but Cassell was still weak and it was just too late. Van Horn ended with 18 points.

The Nets had played well, though, and everyone knew it. Jordan, especially, was impressed, saying, "We never saw a full, healthy New Jersey Nets squad, and I am glad. We took advantage of their situation."

So the Nets' season was over, but the future held a lot of promise. With someone like Van Horn to build a team around, the prospects of other playoff spots over the next several years looked good.

Shortly after the Nets were eliminated from the playoffs, the NBA All-Rookie team was announced. Those selected to the first team were Brevin Knight and Zydrunas Ilgauskas of the Cleveland Cavaliers, Ron Mercer of the Boston Celtics, Tim Duncan of the San Antonio Spurs, and Van Horn.

The Rookie All-Stars are voted for by the league's coaches, and a coach is not allowed to vote for one of his own players. Two points are awarded for a first-team vote and one for a second-team vote, and the maximum a player can receive is 56 points. Both Van Horn and Duncan received the maximum.

Duncan was selected as Rookie of the Year, aided in the vote by the fact that Van Horn missed 20 games due to his injuries. Van Horn, however, was the Nets' leading scorer (19.7), second leading rebounder (6.6), and top free throw shooter (84.6%).

The Nets as a team improved from the dismal

26 wins and 56 losses in 1996-97 to 43-39 with Van Horn, and it was the first time in the team's NBA history (the team was born in the old American Basketball Association) that it didn't fall below .500 during the season. Led by Van Horn, the Nets were the top scoring team in the Eastern Conference. And thanks mainly to Williams, the Nets also led the league in offensive rebounds.

His teammates look to Van Horn as the leader for a future filled with playoffs. Williams spoke for everyone when he said, "Nothing scares him. He wants to go out and play as well as he can every night. He's the first one at practice and the last one to leave. I'm an eight-year veteran, and this kid is helping me with my game and making me better."

Keith Van Horn always gives his all in every game and plans on leading the New Jersey Nets to many more winning seasons.

CHRONOLOGY

1975	Born in Diamond Bar, California, the third child of Kenneth and May Van Horn
1989	Enters Diamond Bar High School
1993	Begins classes at the University of Utah after accepting a basketball scholarship; meets Amy Sida, his future wife
1994	Keith's father, Kenneth Van Horn, dies suddenly of a heart attack
1995	Daughter, Sabrina, born on May 30
1996	Marries Amy
1997	Named consensus All-American as a senior at Utah; drafted by the Philadelphia 76ers as the second overall pick in the NBA draft; traded to the New Jersey Nets
1998	Leads Nets to first playoff appearance in four years; leads Nets in scoring; is unanimous pick for All-Rookie team

STATISTICS

KEITH VAN HORN

College Statistics

Year	Team	G	FGM	FGA	Pct	FTM	FTA	Pct	REB	AST	PTS	AVG
93-94	Utah	25	161	312	.516	100	129	.775	208	21	457	18.3
94-95	Utah	33	246	451	.545	143	167	.856	280	45	694	21.0
95-96	Utah	32	236	439	.538	160	188	.851	283	31	686	21.4
96-97	Utah	32	248	504	.492	151	167	.904	303	45	705	22.0
TOTALS		122	891	1706	.522	554	651	.851	1074	142	2542	20.8

NBA Statistics

Year	Team	G	FGM	FGA	Pct	FTM	FTA	Pct	REB	AST	PTS	AVG
97-98	NJ	62	446	1047	.426	258	305	.846	408	106	1219	19.7

G	games
FGA	field goals attempted
FGM	field goals made
Pct	percent
FTA	free throws attempted
FTM	free throws made
REB	rebounds
AST	assists
PTS	points
AVG	scoring average

FURTHER READING

Calipari, John and Dick Weiss. *Refuse to Lose*. New York: Ballantine Books, 1996.

Harris, Jack C. *The New Jersey Nets*. Mankato, Minn.: Creative Education, 1997.

Jackson, Phil, Charles Barkley, and Gene Siskel. *The Definitive Word on Michael Jordan*. Dallas: Beckett, 1998.

Minsky, Alan. *March to the Finals: The History of College Basketball's Illustrious Final Four*. New York: Metro Books, 1997.

Pluto, Terry. *Loose Balls: The Short, Wild Life of the American Basketball Association as Told by the Players, Coaches, and Movers and Shakers Who Made It Happen*. New York: Fireside, 1991.

ABOUT THE AUTHOR

Brent Kelley is an equine veterinarian and writer. He is the author of eight books on baseball history and two (using the pen name Grant Kendall) on his experiences as a veterinarian. He is a columnist for *Thoroughbred Times*, a weekly horse racing and breeding publication, and *Bourbon Times*, a weekly family newspaper. He has written more than 300 articles for various magazines and newspapers. He lives in Paris, Kentucky, with his wife and children.

INDEX

PHOTO CREDITS
AP/Wide World Photos: pp. 2, 8, 11, 12, 14, 16, 20, 22, 26, 28, 31, 36, 38, 40, 43, 45, 50, 53, 55, 56, 58